The Faithful God . . .

And Why I Choose to Serve Him!

A true and inspiring story of God's faithfulness and love!

Written by Fabrizio Cusson

Published by Fabrizio N. Cusson

ISBN: 978-1466415560

Knowing prescription drug abuse, and the subsequent deep addiction that follows. Seeing how it has grown wildly out of control in recent years. Seeing it has no boundaries, affects people of all ages, genders and social economic status, and because of what I went through. I felt the Lord leading me to write this short book titled, The Faithful God; to encourage others that **there is hope** for them, despite what the world may say. The Faithful God is my testimony of how God saved me, and totally delivered me from this addiction to Oxycontin, Methadone and many other prescription drugs. The book documents many miracles, and the insight God has given me into His love, His grace, His Holy Spirit and how it was the Word of God that caused faith in Jesus to stir inside of me.

You can contact the author by email at:

ThefaithfulGod@yahoo.com

The Faithful God . . .

Introduction

I found myself quietly pondering the past year, placing myself back to before Jesus put His hand on my life. These memories, of a not-so-distant past, are still whirling uncontrollably through my mind. The realization of what has happened is sinking ever deeper into my conscience. I recall, then my mind explodes with an inexpressible joy, a sense of complete satisfaction is strength to my bones. I feel more alive each day that passes. My spirit is rising within me, my soul stands renewed, and physically I'm restored to a day I all but counted as lost. I'm in possession of what I never believed I could own. I ponder in my heart the magnificent meaning to own this experience and delivery. Clearly it's only now that I am able to recount the past and fully appreciate what a gift I have truly been given!

Before this, I've reflected on my past and found only shame. But today as I look back on what could be considered the worse areas of my life, I find myself encouraged. I thank God for who I am today and give no credit toward who I was in the past. I keep my eyes focused clearly on who I will be from here forward, not who I had been. My senses are heightened as I contemplate what God has done in me in the recent past; then I am overwhelmed to consider what He has in store for the future! In my previous state, I never could have imagined such awesome change; I just did not have an insight into what God could do. Today, I could never imagine going back to the way I was. Previously I had all but counted myself out for any positive changes in my life. I fully expected to die young with this deep addiction to prescription painkillers. Had it not been for the multiple and miraculous events that arose all around me, I know I would still be on a destructive course today, or maybe already dead. As overwhelming as all that has transpired seems, I am quite clear on this: Jesus has a different plan for my life! His plan has only begun to unfold for me.

As I have earlier expressed, I'm so excited to see what He has next! During the time before my deliverance of the painkillers and after my first real-life introduction as to who Jesus is, I began to write a journal of my life as I saw it each day. At the time I began journaling, I couldn't have offered a real, clear reason as to what really drove me to start writing my thoughts or even track my life events, seeing how I never really ever wrote about much of anything. Today I smile a bit as my spirit senses the real reason I made my notes. I see that Jesus knew foreknew He was about to do a great miracle by using an accumulation of miracles over a period of time that would deliver me from a ruthless addiction and bring my life into submission to the Father through Him. My notes now written into this short story titled "The Faithful God" will serve as my testimony to others as to why I call Jesus my Savior and why I call my Father in heaven the Faithful God. I want to proclaim out loud what He has done for me! I pray it will help to cause you to reach out for the same real hope He offered me. I know He's willing no matter what your situation may be, yes He is, our Faithful God!

> *I will lift up my eyes to the hills,*
> *from where comes my help?*
> *My help comes from the Lord*
> *who made heaven and earth.*
> (Psalm 121:1)

Chapter 1

For the purpose of my testimony, I will first need to take you back to around 1996, at the time I was twenty-four years old. I had already been married for three years. I was running my own construction / remodel business and enjoying what I considered to be a fairly exciting and adventurous life. I loved my job and enjoyed a respectable income. I always liked to reward my hard work with some whiskey and beer after work. I ditched my wife most every weekend for the bars drinking just to be drunk and carefree. I spent the very minimum amount of time at home to keep my marriage hanging by a thread. I knew my wife was disappointed and somewhat depressed about the way things seemed to be turning out for our marriage. I myself wasn't really concerned about our marriage; whatever happened seemed good with me.

It was a Friday afternoon in December 1996 when a blizzard-type snowstorm hit during a regular workday. Being a Friday, I had to leave work to get paychecks done and delivered for our workers. Leaving the job site, it became obvious very fast I was in for a real slow and dangerous ride. Within a mile of the job, the road became unmanageable as I fishtailed down a hill into a large tree. I was struck on the back of head and neck with two steel levels I had hanging on a gun rack behind me. I felt a sting and some intermittent pain as I worked to get the smashed door to open. A city plow truck witnessing the wreck, called in for an ambulance, and insisted I sit still as I was holding my neck, warning me I could have a spinal injury. I was agitated as he insisted I sit around waiting for this ambulance. I just wanted to call a worker of mine who was just up the road and hitch a ride back to the job site to gather my thoughts. The ambulance arrived and began to make a big fuss over me. I admitted I had a little neck pain and some numbness, but I felt I would be fine. They aggressively insisted because of the truck's twisted condition and the impact it took, that I should be brought to the hospital for x-rays. I finally gave in; thinking a ride to the hospital had to be better than standing around contemplating my answer. I remember lying in a hallway outside the x-ray department with stretchers lined up in a row; there were so many accidents all at once the hospital was running out of room for their patients. From my stretcher I heard one of the radiologists call for a doctor to come to the x-ray room as soon as possible.

I lay there in a brace, which did not allow me to look side to side, but I knew the doctor had arrived when I heard them talking. He seemed to be reviewing an x-ray when he asked, "Where is the patient?" I heard the reply: "He's in the hallway in a stretcher." The doctor requested placing this patient in a room immediately for further evaluation. I remember thinking how lucky I was not to be that patient. Just then a doctor came out and informed me that I had C-1 through C-2 fracture(s), which could be dangerous and moving wrong could mean being paralyzed from the head down. They quickly brought me to a room and went through all the motions. It was later determined that I could possibly have had this injury from childbirth, that it may have healed itself and was inevitably reinjured in this accident, or that it was a fresh break. It was too hard for them to tell for sure, but nevertheless, it needed to be dealt with.

There was some talk in the room by a couple doctors about how fortunate I was not to be paralyzed. Other than some numbness and tingling, I felt OK. They seemed very concerned. Myself, I just wanted to go home, I had heard enough already. I really just wanted a stiff drink and a nap. I was sent to a neurosurgeon; my neck was braced, and I immediately began taking a pain medicine called Percocet 5 mg, one or two every eight hours to dull some light pain. I clearly remember going in for surgery; all I could think about was when I could get back to work. I also remember waking up having never felt any such pain in my life. I just never realized that any human could be capable of feeling anything like it. I always figured so much pain would cause you to pass out, but I was wide-awake. I complained about the pain for days. I learned quickly complaining meant I would be given another shot of morphine or Demerol to relieve the symptoms. I can remember my wife sitting next to my bed pressing the IV button every five minutes for more pain medicine in between the shots. It allowed me to sleep without having to wake up from the pain. It was later that week, thinking back to how awful the initial pain was, when I realized for the first time how much my wife really loved me. She sat in the hard plastic chair while I slept, always smiling when I woke up. I knew then that I could always count on her to be there no matter what the situation is. It's funny how it took that for me to see her commitment, but it was the first time I honestly realized it.

Chapter 2

Leaving the hospital a week later I was prescribed more painkillers in the form of Percocet 5 mg tabs and Valium for the tension in my muscles. I truly needed them and used them as I wished. About two 5 mg tabs every four hours. This went on for months. I did realize at one point that my pain had been steadily subsiding, but I still felt I wanted the meds. Lying on the couch for nine months did not help, but this was the time I needed for a good healing in my spine, so I continued through those months back and forth to the doctors getting more pills and x-rays.

Eventually I was able to get back to work, which I loved so much. As a builder, I got to work with new people all the time and take on projects that always made me feel challenged and important by my subcontractors and clients. When I was out, I turned the business over fully to a good friend and partner who personally delivered all the checks and paperwork to me each week. He was a great friend, whom I trusted explicitly. He had an incredible heart, but he was also stretched very thin, and there was no way he could perfectly do both of our jobs at the same time. So we did the best we could, with what we had. When I returned to work, I retained my best clients but lost some also. It became apparent the business just wasn't the same. I remember reminiscing of all the good times we had, teaming up on some of the most impossible predicaments and coming out at the end of each day smelling like a rose and a few dollars richer. It seemed like the whole crew had parted their way, and it was all too sad to see how it had changed so much. I began to rely on the pain medication to dull a mild depression that slowly became more and more profound. I began to notice the medicine was giving me a euphoric feeling, and I was well on my way to really enjoying that euphoria. At this point, I still had some minor head and neck pain on a daily basis, but I was way past the time I should have been kept on narcotic pain medicine. It wasn't long until I closed up the company and went into a new business adventure selling cars. It was better because I spent a lot of time in an office versus job sites, roofs, and ladders. My wife and I both thought it would be better for my neck and the pain, and ultimately we were right. The physical part of selling cars was much less burdensome to me. On the other hand, I had a lot more time to think about nothing between sales, to actually search for my pain and feel it. After all it was pain that always justified the pills for me, so if I felt I had pain, even a little pain, I could take the medication without guilt. The fact a major side effect of the pill was euphoria, wasn't my fault, even if I liked it and looked forward to it so very much. I was building tolerance to the drug, so I saw my doctor, and he prescribed me a new, more powerful drug called OxyContin. I was prescribed 10 mg three times a day, which was double the dosage of what I was using. Within a few days, I complained about the new dose not being enough, and so I was given an increase to 20 mg three times a day. I liked this much better; this new dose was giving me a much warmer euphoric feeling and I was instantly in love. My depression actually started to sink away and life seemed to get better. So much so, it wasn't long before I closed up the car dealership and went back to being what I loved, a builder and salesman; clutching tightly to the pills wherever I went—to a point I was obsessive about them. I continually worried about them being lost or stolen, counting them daily to see how many were left and so on. I just loved the warm feeling, the euphoria, the absolute high and happiness they seemed to be giving me.

Chapter 3

A year or two passed when I was offered a great-paying job selling for a national insurance contractor, and I decided to go for it. I kept my own business but downsized it considerably. I was driven by a hunger for money and status. Before I knew it, I was overloaded and was working seven days a week to pay bills and live like I wanted to. By now my pill use went from 15 mg (three Percocet's) a day in the beginning to about 360 mg (which is equivalent to seventy-two Percocet's a day without Tylenol mixed in), and most days, I used more than I was prescribed. I always found ways to get my refills early. If the early refill wouldn't work, I had a network of people that would sell them to me for $20 a pill. Buying them would cost me at the time about $200 per day. I still did not look at myself as an abuser. I liked the idea I could get this warm euphoric high and blame it on pain. I realize now that any pain I had was caused by overworking, never resting, chain-smoking, drinking and the fact I needed this pain to justify the addiction.

I quickly forgot about my wife's commitment to me while in recovery, and before long I began to really despise her. I couldn't stand the way she thought she could tell me how I needed to make changes. My mother, who was a Christian, was witnessing to her and bringing her to church; and it apparently was having some effect on her ideals. Myself, I was happy to stay where I was. My daughter wanted more of my attention, and I knew I had to give it to her, but I just was not able to make a real effort to be a great dad. I was just this below-average, pill-popping, whiskey-drinking type of dad. I did the absolute minimum, just enough to get by and keep outward appearances looking reasonable. Even worse for me, my pills were not making me high any longer; taking them became more of a way for me to stay normal and remain free from any withdrawals. I continually chased that euphoric feeling I loved so much, but it was getting much more difficult. The euphoric high came fewer and further between each dose, sometimes weeks before I'd feel high again. Many times I would convince myself to take a larger dose to see if that would bring the euphoric feeling back. If the increased experimental dose worked and I got euphoric feelings, then I would never be able to allow myself to return to the lower dose again. The doses were getting above what my health insurance considered normal, and they stopped covering my prescriptions after a certain point each year, which meant I had to pay about $1,500 per month myself to keep normal. I made sure I always had the cash ready for that script. It was pills first, bills later. I remember hearing my wife on the phone arranging with our pharmacy for a charge account. I thought how pathetic this really had become, but I still had no clear idea of what I was really doing to myself and my family.

Chapter 4

In 2000 (within four years of my first pill) I began having more health issues. I was experiencing these extreme hot flashes, terrible stomach pains, uncontrollable fatigue, horrific irritability, etc. The irritability was just not normal at all. If anyone even looked at me wrong, anywhere, anytime I was ready to explode. Other times I would just black out while people were speaking to me; this all happened on a daily basis. I remember my wife fully convinced herself, telling me she went online and she was sure I had narcolepsy, a sleeping disorder. I went to a few specialists for exams and tests. At one point my doctor felt we might have discovered a problem, when I had been given surgery for my gallbladder to be removed, but the symptoms did not change. I had countless day surgeries for nerve blocks, Botox injections, and epidurals to a point I was going in twice a week. Looking back I realize all these injections and surgeries was the source of any pain I had. It took at least three to four days to heal from each round of injections. But without the pain, I couldn't justify the pills, so I stayed the course. I had other surgeries on my scalp, the top of my head to have part of my occipital nerve severed to help alleviate any head pain from the hundreds of injections I had. It may have helped with any pain but it left a large portion of my head and face completely numb, which was worse than having pain! What were these doctors thinking?

I was forced to quit drinking all together because of the drug interaction. At first I was indecisive about not drinking, but as long as I kept the pills, I agreed to the loss of alcohol. Nothing I did changed the symptoms; they only got worse. I knew I had to make a decision when the symptoms got so bad that I couldn't tell if I'd snap on someone or just pass out while driving. I needed to get my life in order and get back to my old self. I met with a leading neurologist in Boston, and he scheduled me for surgery to cut off more of my nerves in the area of the damage and remove the screws in my spine, which may have been causing an irritation. I remember waking up from the surgery and screaming in pain. I was told later that the nurses were baffled. They had given me so much medication the first hour I awoke that they believed I would die of an overdose if I received anything else. My family was asking them to help me, and they were just not comfortable to give me any more medicine. They claimed to have never seen anyone that could have so much intravenous medication and have no reaction at all. They called in a special team of anesthesiologist called the A-team. They worked with me in the recovery room and discovered the problem I was having. They said I was getting dangerously immune to pain medicine, and this was why my pain was so intolerable because my body had stopped making its own natural pain medicine. I was hooked up to a drug cocktail that was either rarely or never used by this team before. Several different, highly potent intravenous medicines, simultaneously, at large doses for two days straight until I was slowly weaned down to lesser amounts. Before I left, these doctors had taken an interest in me and my tolerance and wanted to learn more about my situation.

When the interview was done, they handed me a business card and informed me that I needed professional help to get off this medicine. After recovery from the surgery, I searched for a rehab center to address their concerns. In early 2001, I was admitted to a widely known rehab center in Boston. I went in feeling good and ready to make the change. My intake interview with the rehab doc went well, and they explained how they would try to take me down and send me home in thirty days drug free, and with coping skills for any pain I may have.

Week one was pure hell, sweating, vomiting, aches like I never knew existed, and other symptoms I wouldn't mention. Week two was just as bad or worse, but I was slowly progressing down the road of freedom from medicine while learning ways of coping and living without pills. By the middle of week three, I had these terrible body aches that went down my spine into my back and chest. My doctors came in my room and administered aspirin in case it was heart related and some other meds. I remember demanding to my doctor to prescribe me some OxyContin. They reasoned with me, but I wanted nothing to do with reason: "Just give me back my life!" I said, "I'll accept the risk and learn to love it even if I am an irritable zombie, slurring my words and feeling perpetually terrible."

This one doctor stayed behind and haggled with me for some time, explaining to me that my body had stopped making its own endorphins and other chemicals years ago, and any little pain would seem like a big one, especially now that I was withdrawing from such heavy use of Oxycontin. It was explained to me that another symptom of withdrawal was increased pain sensitivity. Because of my previous injury, there were very few doctors willing to refuse me if I asked for medicine and I knew it. Rather than stay the course, I remained on a low dose of methadone and oxycodone, which they were already using to withdraw me. So I left the fourth week on methadone and six Percocet's a day, which was hardly anything to write home about, a much-lower dose yes, but also enough to ease the pain of the withdrawals. The scary thing was that I was just so happy and relieved to still have my pills. I could keep some medicine, and it felt so good to be me.

Chapter 5

Within a few weeks of being home, the honeymoon was over. I was still experiencing terrible withdrawals from the lower dose. I wanted more; I wanted to feel warm and euphoric, to do away with the sleeplessness and restlessness. I set an appointment with my doctor, and he prescribed me my favorite pill—OxyContin. My depression was gone, literally gone in one day. I went from wanting to die… to can't wait to live on! My new symptoms included happiness and fulfillment. I was tolerable again for my family; everything seemed so great. Though as before, it didn't last long, within a month it was all back. Slurred speech, stomach pains, dizziness, nightmares, severe sweating, chest pains, headaches, irritability, black outs and a newer and deeper depression that I had not yet known. Maybe I realized I had failed the rehab, or maybe the drug was really beginning to take its full toll on my body. I continued this way for four more years, increasing my dose from every six months to every three months to every three or four weeks until I reached about 1,000 mg a day. I had already stopped swallowing the pills and began crushing them to break the time release, looking for instant results. I made countless trips to the hospital for my heart, headaches, and severe nausea. I was waking up at night gasping for air because I was so relaxed from the medicine that I would forget to breathe. Every single night my wife would have to literary shake and hit me until I would awaken from these horrific nightmares; where I'd be stuck in my sleep, fully aware mentally, but completely paralyzed physically. I had no more ideas other than to take more and more pills and try chasing it away with euphoria. One evening in mid to late 2004, I had this crippling fear that came over me as I was leaning against my dresser. I had opened my drawer full of pills to make myself a dose, as I wrestled the child proof cover off; I dropped a new bottle on the floor. I remember absolutely panicking as I watched one hundred 80 mg pills go in every direction, under the bed, the dresser, out the bedroom door, etc. I scrambled to the floor, crawling in desperation to find each and every last one, despite this unusually painful migraine calling me back to my feet. I fought the intense pain until each one was found. Just then a realization hit me so clearly; I'd rather die than lose a single dose. I felt this reality of impending doom fill me up to the core of my being, fear flooded over me like I had never experienced. My heart was racing so fast just then, I couldn't catch my breath. I was feeling perpetually weakened, like someone just pulled the plug on me and all the life within me was spilling out uncontrollably. I had been fearful many times in life with all that was happening, but this was different—it felt too real and my mind would not stop racing . . . thinking of death. It was this same night I stayed up just worrying and being fearful of everything bad that could happen and most likely will if I stayed this course. The real fear set in deep when I began to tell myself that I was never going to be able to break free of these pills or the intense pull of the addiction. I feared I was going to lose my family, my business, my life. I remember telling my wife the next morning I thought I may have really finally cracked, literally just gone insane inside. I sat alone for hours contemplating what it would be like if I were to end up in a mental institution for this, it was all just getting too intolerable for me to bear. It was uncontrollable, a consuming fear like I never had experienced. I prepared for matters to get worse very fast. I pumped myself up with a dose and went to work, thinking what have I done to my kids, my wife—who stood by me all these days, tirelessly waiting by my bedside, surgery after surgery, disappointment on top of disappointment. She stood by me when I was out of work, when we nearly lost our home, depleted our savings, through all my mood swings, sleeping my life away while she ran the home and cared for our children. I thought of how cheap of a husband and father I had become to be just sucking the life out of my family because I was an addict and gave so little in return to them. I was nearly incapacitated by this fear, and I had no idea who to turn to.

Chapter 6

I could not sleep, I was unable to eat, concentrate, or just plain function at all. I just had full-time thoughts of death and destruction racing through my head twenty-four hours a day. I knew seeing a doctor would just mean another and more medicine. By then I was already taking powerful antidepressants and several other potent medications for some time, and I knew another painkiller increase would very well kill me. I had only one place left to turn. In my mind it was a real long shot, and even if it would work, I certainly was not deserving of relief of any kind. Growing up in a Christian family I was taught about God, how Jesus came to this earth to die for our sins and make our lives whole again. I knew all the popular stories about Moses and Jonah, turning bread into wine and so forth . . .

Call to Me, and I will answer you, and
show you great and mighty things ... (Jeremiah 33:3).

I jostled with the idea of praying, but kept telling myself Jesus might not even be real. For years I had fought myself on the fact that Jesus may be a man-made story for our own happiness. I had little to no faith in Jesus or God, and I felt even if He was real I wasn't worthy of His time. Then while thinking of these doubts in my mind, I remembered something that happened to me when I was a small child lying in bed in my parents' room. I had an urge to lift my head and turn it toward the window; when I did I saw what I believed was Mary the mother of Jesus, holding a small child in her hand surrounded by bright colors and light. She smiled at me as she stared. I was so scared that I quickly turned away and buried my head in the pillow; slowly I brought up the nerve to look again to see if she was still looking, and when I did she was gone.

All my life I never forgot that experience, and it had a big impact on my thinking because I knew without any doubt what I had seen and experienced. By my teenage years, I buried it as a childish fantasy, but deep down inside I always knew what happened was real. So I decided to pray, I very simply asked Jesus to help me believe in Him, to lead me free of this misery, to give me faith in His existence. I knew for certain this world had nothing more to offer me, so this was my last chance of any positive change. To this point I had literally exhausted every doctor, hospital room, medication, and remedy man had to offer me. Surely my next stop was my grave. My prayer to Jesus wasn't so much that I was looking for assistance to be done with pills; I was convinced by all that I heard, read, and seen that I was undoubtedly hooked for life. The reality of my prayer was more my own preparation for death, thinking if there truly is a hell, I definitely don't want to go there. Of course, I wanted to be free of the terrible symptoms I was experiencing. I wanted to be free of the fears and depression I was in, but the euphoria I got from the pills was the real love of my life, and I didn't want to lose that. I wanted to keep the pills and loose the symptoms of my daily overdosing, my thinking was, if I died getting high then I'd at least I'd go to heaven not hell. Even with this sense of death all around me, I still wasn't willing to lose any chance of a single moment of euphoria. Prayer seemed to help at first, but I was quickly falling back into the same routines, the depression, anxiety and fear I had was like nothing I can explain. Then one night I had a dream about an old friend, which prompted me to begin having reminiscing and racing thoughts of all my old friends and the days of heavy drug use. The cocaine parties, the drunkenness and so on . . . and it just made me sick thinking that many of my friends were still entrenched deep in the ruts of addiction. I was actually telling myself how fortunate I was to have gotten into the construction business when I did, leaving them all behind. I was just so blind, and it is real sad to look back and think that I was actually that arrogant to not see I had become no different, probably worse. The person I dreamt about was an old and very close friend who left with me as a teenager to Florida; we were both fifteen years old and together we lived for a life of drugs and alcohol. Toward the end of my time in Florida, we were literary being hunted by two very mean Mexican immigrants over a bad deal. Fearing for my life, I called my parents and left Florida on the next plane back to New Hampshire, but my friend stayed. My last contact with him was more then ten years earlier. I had lost all communication with him and had no idea where he was. So back to the dream!

It was about this old friend being in front of a judge who was sentencing him to a long prison term, and while he pleaded for another chance, I walked in and pleaded on his behalf. I promised the judge I would vouch on his behalf and keep him clean if he could just have another chance at freedom. The judge reluctantly agreed. I was given full custody of my good old friend! As we were leaving the court, he stole a car! I was very angry with him I couldn't believe he had not learned his lesson. I tried earnestly to stop him, to try and correct his behavior, but he just wouldn't listen to me. I was terrified of how the judge would hold me responsible for him. I figured the judge would have me put in jail with him. At that moment, a loud thud from outside awoke me from my sleep, and I was awake in bed sweating. I just lay there, rustled and restless by this vivid dream. I began wondering, what if he did need my help. What if he's in trouble, I thought? My heart was suddenly and strangely aching for him. The dream was so strikingly real, so vivid. I thought seeing how I was starting to pray lately; maybe I should get out of bed and pray for him.

I knelt on my knees in the family room, and I asked God to help me understand this dream or at least show me if I was just imagining my friend was in some kind of trouble. Right then this overwhelming amount of doubt rushed into my mind, I thought to myself, I must be plumb crazy! I asked myself, what are you doing? Telling myself it was just a dream, just because you had a dream doesn't mean that it's true...get up and go back to sleep before someone sees you! I considered how strange I had been getting lately, I asked myself, "What in the world are you doing?" Sarcasm always won the day with me, and this was no exception. Then the thought came to me, I do not even have his number, so why would I pray for him? I can't even call him and see for myself if he really does need some help. So I stood up from this prayer and I spoke out loud, "Well, God, if you want me to talk with him, give me his number, after all you're God, and they say you can do anything." I went to bed and slept well the rest of the night. The next morning my wife and I drank coffee before I left for work, and she asked me where I had gone the night before. I explained the strange dream I had and my prayer and how I shrugged it off by asking God for his phone number. I really was embarrassed to admit to her that I had prayed, but for some reason it just came out and I told her. Just moments after I told her, my five-year-old son ran in the room, as he did each morning, with my cell phone. He turned it on and said, "Here's your phone for work, Daddy." I thanked him and set it down only to hear a distinct ringtone that meant I had a voice mail message. I immediately checked the message and I was in complete disbelief. Yes, it was my old friend that I dreamt about; he had somehow gotten my number from his friend or relative in New Hampshire who had gotten it from a business ad in the local newspaper! He was obviously under the influence of drugs as he slurred his way through his message. Regardless of his condition, he did manage to leave his phone number and asked me to call him back.

My wife must have seen my expression because she stared at me as she was saying, "What? Who was it?" I just looked at her for a moment and then I said, "I'm not sure you'll believe me if I told you." She persisted and I explained I had just gotten a message from the friend I had dreamt and prayed about . . . and he left me his phone number! She was white as a ghost, and I was completely speechless. This couldn't be true. It must be some type of mistake or coincidence; is someone playing a joke on me, I thought? How could this possibly happen? As much disbelief as I tried to conjure up to explain it all away, I couldn't. I simply could not deny it. It was actually a little frightening how this had just happened. I was brought to a point of complete silence in my mind, just a mind numbing silence. I had only finished telling her the dream minutes earlier. It was such an awkward moment for us both. I was literally left speechless. I never had God work with me like this; it was so prompt, so obviously Him. I quietly reasoned, then realized only God could do this, there was no other explanation. I sensed He was teaching me a valuable lesson in faith. He took my comment "If you're God, you can give me his number." And clearly replied I am God.

Chapter 7

I called this friend back; we talked for a long time. I realized he was in pretty bad shape. We helped him out financially, then flew him to New Hampshire, rented him a place to live, attempting to encourage him to straighten his life out. During the time he was with us, I saw this very sick man. He was not anything like I had remembered. He was a literal disaster waiting to explode any moment. The first day he was with us he was hauled off to a local hospital by ambulance when I found him on the floor having a seizure. He was drooling and spitting all over himself and completely incoherent. I thought he might die at one moment while we awaited the medics. The doctor later explained that he was involved with so many drugs at once that he was at risk of more seizures. My wife and I were a complete wreck at the thought of having to babysit him. From there every day or so disaster did strike him throughout the year; it was very pathetic to watch him like this. On another hand, he held so much promise and talent; he was very likable and fun to be with when he wasn't smashed. I watched him like this for a month or so, and for some reason or the other, he played part in inspiring me to at least try to read the Bible a little. Partly because my mother had convinced him to attend her church every Sunday and he was showing signs of enjoying it. He used to tease me and egg me on every day, saying, "Why won't you go with us, after all you're the one with the dreams from God, right?" He received a Bible and asked me questions about it. I was trying so hard to inspire him, but I didn't know much about the bible.

I think he may have been showing interest in good things to soften me for bad things that he really wanted. He was very cunning, and I was quite pathetic as well. He knew that I wanted for him to be better and ultimately he may have used that against me. I knew I was a bad influence for him because I was giving him some of my pills. When it came right down to it, I knew that he was unstoppable whether or not I would keep obliging his pill problem.

Eventually, he found his own doctor and began the lie that he was in a car accident as a kid; he told the doctors about how painful his back was getting to be. Before I knew it, he was getting his own pills and anything else he could get a hold of. Despite all this, his church attendance, Bible reading and questions did motivate me start to really looking at the Bible more seriously. For that reason, and also the dream I had about him and the related phone number incident, it just seemed to really stick with me. It was still a little unbelievable for me to think it really happened the way it did, but it really did, and I knew it without a doubt. I kept asking my wife, why God would have me get him up here to see him do this to himself. My wife had no patience for him at all because she saw right through him and his lies. But because of the dream God gave me, I was unable to give up on him. Despite how much money he was costing us, the time away from my family to be with him, and the feelings of my wife . . . we couldn't take our eyes of the fact I had this dream and got his phone number the way I did. It was really a turning point for me, but I just was not grasping what God meant by it.

Once I started seriously reading the Bible, the words of God began to take effect. It was the true beginning of my relationship with Christ, but I had no idea what a relationship with Christ really meant for me. At the time I never knew why God had brought my friend to New Hampshire only to see him fail miserably and return to Florida . . . after so much time, money, and effort. But now I can look back and see that it was a turning point for me. I was able to see skid row close up, a face-to-face look in the mirror that no other mirror was able to show me. It was me I saw in that mirror. He was in no doubt in worse shape than I was; I was barely functioning, and he was completely dysfunctional. It would have only taken some awkward circumstance to arise, and I would have been just like him or worse, dead. I believe this was why I had so much fear building up in me because deep down I knew I was swiftly losing control of my life. Although I began praying and reading the Bible, I was still dealing with this consuming addiction and its affects on my being. My tolerance was running thin. My anger was building. I was sickly and on the verge of a complete disaster, and I knew it was near. Fear gripped me and ruled me, but it also was the vehicle that drove me to the only thing left for me to turn to—that was Jesus.

Chapter 8

Come to Me, all you who labor and are heavy laden, and I will give you rest…

I began to read the Bible more and more each day, I was desperately seeking for this Jesus to reveal Himself to me. In the midst of this my habit worsened, I continually found myself convincing my doctor for more and more medicine. I was running out a week or two early every month. My dosage was so high I stopped counting. In comparison to the Percocet 5 mg, which was where this all started, I was now chewing and abusing the equal of over two hundred of these pills each day or 1,000 mg of OxyContin a day in its pure form without the Tylenol mixed in. As close to God as I got, I was haunted with past memories of rehab years earlier. I wrestled with an impending sense of doom, destined to be an addict the rest of my life. I knew that I had to get my life right with Jesus, at least when I die I'd be going up, not down. I fully expected a fairly short life span and felt I should prepare for this addiction to take the next step and kill me.

One evening, in the early spring of 2005, I had lain in bed to rest my eyes and get away from the stress of the day. I felt myself slipping away into a trancelike state. I believe I was not fully asleep nor was I awake. I heard a voice calling to me. I was conscious and in complete darkness. I could not see anything, but I heard this voice calling out. Suddenly I was overcome with an incredible draw toward the voice, it was Jesus calling me.

I recall Jesus speaking to me, saying, "Look at my face, you have to come to Me, you're lost in darkness and you cannot see in it. Come to Me and you'll see through My light." I also recall saying these things from my own mouth as well, almost like I was prophesying or ministering to myself and others around me. I walked toward Him and as I did I heard these voices in my mind telling me my loan payments were overdue, and a house we had built was not closing on schedule. I began to think about money and the worries of my life. Just then Jesus showed me that I needed to focus on His face—look at My face and to turn your life over completely to Me, surrender. At that moment I was in His presence, and I was so filled with such a complete peace, no doubt this was of God. Then I realized Jesus was crying and very sorrowful. As I looked around, He revealed to me why He was weeping. There were countless millions of people wandering about in darkness; they seemed so alone and very afraid, so completely lost, hopeless, and desperate for some direction. Then I too began to feel such a great despair for them; they had no idea Jesus was right there with them! I began to cry out to them, to explain Jesus was right here, they could turn to him! I wondered why they could not see Him as I did. I was trying to make them see the truth of Jesus. He's right here! Just look at His face! It will be all right if you come to Him! My heart was so struck by these people I wanted them so badly to see the peace I had in His presence so they could experience it for themselves.

Right then I heard that voice telling me that we had a major problem on a job, and I was needed right away. I just did not want to leave, but this voice persisted, telling me if I did not go my business would be at risk. My worse fear was always to lose control of my finances, my job, and my family's security, so I began to worry and consider the need to leave. As I contemplated my worldly concerns, I began to come out of the trancelike state I was in. As I did I heard or spoke these words, "Look at His face, turn to Jesus the rest will work itself out." I knew the people in the darkness were resisting this concept of turning to Jesus, and I was telling them, "Just look at the face of Jesus!" I suddenly became awake and alert. I was lying in bed, my body was shivering but I was not cold. I was in peace, but at the same time I knew with all my heart I needed to make a change in my life. It became obvious to me that Jesus just showed me very clearly that I was one of these lost souls / people wandering in the darkness of the world. My heart was just aching for the other people and myself who were all lost in this utter darkness; they walked around so aimlessly, trying so hard, looking for something but never finding it. I just knew I also was aimless in the dark with them. I wanted to be back so badly in that peaceful state with Jesus Christ. I saw the futility of man from His standpoint. The needless pain, anguish, and misery mankind has caused themselves by seeking the world rather than His face. I didn't want to be wandering in darkness when all the while Jesus was right there. I just needed to seek His face!

Of course, somewhat naturally for me at this point in my life, I doubted soon after the whole experience that I had not just conjured this up in my mind somehow or that the drugs I was taking somehow paralyzed me into this trance-type state. I knew it happened, but I wasn't finding myself taking the steps to accept the message Jesus gave to me. Between the dream I had and the following phone call experience related to the dream, and now this experience, I was considering the possibility of going to church, at least once to see what I was missing, if anything. My mom being a believer all my life invited us year after year to her church and I knew the pastor, so I decided that Sunday I'd go. It was very hard for me to make the decision to go. I had a false understanding of what church really was like. I viewed all churches based on what mistakes I have seen other Christians make. Jesus began showing me not to blame God for what man has done to me or others. I had to just look to Jesus and leave the rest behind. I had always understood God to be this firm ruler, who was very angry at us all, especially me. Now after the experience I just had with Jesus weeping and crying, there was this growing feeling in me that I may have been misunderstanding God altogether. So that Sunday, my family and I went to church for the first time in years.

Chapter 9

Going to church seemed so awkward! First there was singing, which was fine, and the people were all very nice. It may have felt very awkward because I know my mother had told many people about me. Those thoughts that people may know my business made me angry. I sat there with my anger and frustration growing. Finally the pastor came on to preach. I thought to myself, it's about time! I had already fully decided this would be the last time I'd be going to church for a while. I hardly cared to listen, but I did. I was taken aback when he got up and said he was going to preach on something else but this "Holy Spirit" of his had somehow put it on his heart to preach on the *face of Jesus.* He began his sermon by stressing the importance of looking at the face of Jesus, in any circumstance, in any need we could always look at the face of

Jesus for help and salvation. I'll admit he had my full attention by that time . . . what really took me back was when he talked about life's circumstances, how they tend to take our focus off the face of Jesus.

The pastor explained how we use excuses, how we are responsible for things on earth and therefore we take eyes off Jesus and take matters into our own hands. Because of this we lose sight of Him, fall into the darkness of the world, and become blinded and hardened. Meanwhile Jesus weeps for us to come to Him, and we just don't seem to listen. I knew Jesus was talking to me, very clearly explaining to me that I did not conjure this up in my mind—it was from Him.

It seems to me He was also confirming that I could not do this on my own, that I needed to look for Him and I'll find Him. I needed to knock and the door would be opened. I needed to just ask and I would receive. What a concept, I thought. I could ask and I'll receive it! So I asked, I sought Him, and I knocked and I knocked some more. And each day after that Sunday I was changed a little more into someone I never knew I could be! Within weeks of this sermon, I had fully dove into the Bible. I read the New Testament within a couple months and then reread lots of it two and three times. Each night for hours, admittedly somewhat neglecting my family, I was completely entrenched in what God's word for me was that day, and I was lifted to a joy I never felt before. All my fear was completely gone, and I knew He opened the door for me, and He let me come in—the rest was up to me to accept His offer. Through His strength, I was beginning to see it was an offer I could take Him up on. I was still taking the pills bad as ever, but many other things changed. I smiled and was happy. I stopped swearing almost immediately (which was very hard for me). I became more compassionate toward my family and friends. I felt a fire burning in me for Jesus like I could never forget. At any moment with no control over it, I would well up in tears at the thought of how much I loved Jesus and what He did for me on the cross. So many changes happened in a few short months just this alone was a *major miracle* in my life. Although I was still on the meds, I was finding less joy in them and more in Christ. The love of my life, pills was becoming the hate of my life; Christ was taking its place. He was becoming my new euphoria!

"So then faith comes by hearing, and hearing by the word of God"
(Rom. 10:17)

Chapter 10

You shall know the truth and the truth shall set you free...

One evening I went down to the pill draw and began to crush my dose, and I felt so sad and sickly, not physically sick . . . just sick and tired of the unending addiction. I could not handle it anymore. I wanted out and I set my mind right there I would look to Christ for a complete 100 percent healing of my addiction to pills. I recalled a story in the book of Matthew that struck me, where a leper said to Jesus, "Lord if you are willing you could make me clean," and Jesus responded, "I am willing." And he was immediately healed. I just loved that saying, "I am willing" so much that I kept telling myself He's willing, and it kept me on course to start to build up my faith and trust in Christ.

He Is Willing!

At first I was energized and ready. I was ready for a complete miracle, and then the reality set in, or doubt, either way, I was so scared and I knew the terror I faced. My business could not withstand me out of work for so long. Besides my wife and my friend from Florida, the rest of my family and friends did not know I was still taking these pills because I had been lying to them for more than four years that I was clean out of the rehab center in 2001. I asked myself how I would explain this.

I knew even if I told everyone the truth about me I still could never leave another month to go do a rehab. It had to be done like business as usual. So I prayed and I asked the Lord to help me, but I continued out of fear to stay the course of seeking Jesus and taking pills. Instead of being smashed and angry, I was smashed and hopeful. One evening I read the story of David and Goliath. I really was struck by the way David was so sure, so positive, that he would and could slay a giant, and how he took charge of the situation; he left the armor of King Saul behind and took a slingshot and a few stones with no fear or concern. He just trusted in God and he overcame such a huge obstacle. It inspired me greatly, and I began to think of the story of Moses and how God had brought the Jews out of Egypt with such mighty works and miracles. It was a long road in the desert because of their lack of faith, but nevertheless, He brought them out of bondage and into freedom. The people of Israel actually began to complain that life in Egypt, although in bondage, was better for them because there was no guesswork involved; they knew they had food day to day and water, but in the desert they had to rely on God for food and water. The more God performed His miracles, it seemed the more they complained. It seemed that no matter what God would do, they just did not see it. I thought to myself, are these people blind or what? Then it hit me, yes they were blind and so are you! The Lord had changed my life drastically and daily. He gave me a dream that was awe-inspiring, a vision that was confirmed, and I was being uplifted out of depression!

So many things began to happen for the good in me and my family. All the changes were the evidence of his glory taking over my life. People I knew very well would actually come to me and say, "You're different; you're always whistling and smiling, what's changed?" I noticed that I was having a positive effect on people without even trying. In spite of the changes, I wasn't taking the step of faith to make the change over my addiction. I liked it safe where I was, taking pills and being happy at the same time. I liked the joy of Christ and the comforts of the world. I know now I was being convicted by the Holy Spirit to press forward in my growth. I guess this is what I meant when I said I had no idea the effect a relationship with Christ would have on me. The more I thought about taking the pills, the more I'd lose the joy I had been building up for months. So I had a choice, the sense of a momentary joy of these pills or the true and lasting joy of Jesus. I set a date to make a change, called my doctor, and met with him. I told him I wanted a change of medicine to methadone for withdrawals, and I was getting off the OxyContin. He looked at me funny, and I know he did not believe me. He gave me the "it is going to be a really hard road" speech, "don't expect it to be quick . . . this may take longer than you realize." So I asked how long, and he replied, "Six to nine months at least, probably longer, depending on you, maybe never." He knew I was deeply addicted. He explained after the physical withdrawals that it will be a forever mental battle to overcome the pull toward and desire for the pills. I left still feeling OK, but worried!

I stuck to the decision, and the next day I started the change. Although I was dreading it terribly, I expected God would deliver me in a few weeks or less, maybe even immediately. I not only had to deal with the withdrawal side, but I had to also cope with the reality of not feeling euphoric anymore . . . all the while keeping my composure and not missing any work. Another strange thing and I do not know why, but my spirit just was unable to involve my doctor anymore. He seemed to portray that I would never make it, and that I was just buckling under pressure to be off the medicine because of its bad name with people. I knew he was not going to be much help when he patted me on the back on my way out the door and, with a smile said, "Good luck!" I knew my faith was growing, I could feel it inside more and more each day. I knew then that God would take the glory for this, not my doctor. I refused to use him anymore or ask for Valium or any other meds that supposedly helped with withdrawal symptoms. Other than a very brief and required checkup months later, because of the Methadone prescription, I have never seen or spoke to him again. I knew from rehab that even with all these meds, withdrawal was still going to be unbearable anyway. I just needed to look to the face of Jesus, I knew He was willing. I just wanted Jesus, and I believe that's exactly how He had planned it from the start. I kept telling myself, He's willing . . .

Chapter 11

I began the taper on November 2, 2005. I immediately began to get very sick and very mean, within just hours I was falling apart from every side. I was agitated, anxious, emotional, and physically sick. It was very difficult to even be around other people, but I forced myself to deal. I recall at the beginning of the second week of withdrawals, when I was trying to get some work done in my home office. The symptoms of withdrawals were so difficult—my heart was pounding, I was short of breath, I was sweating terribly, emotionally and physically jumping out of my skin while running back and forth to the bathroom. Through all that I was under, the pressure of having to hold myself together for the business and my family, I asked Jesus for peace, I prayed for help . . . and I questioned why I was feeling so sick. I truly believed God was going to make this really easy for me. But right then He showed me that I actually had it pretty good considering the situation. You see as hard as it was I was still working every day, earning money for the household and business, managing my customers, being a father and a husband all the while withdrawing. I was seeing how He had allowed me to function as I had necessity, but at the same time, He allowed me to experience the consequence of my addiction. Yes, I was very sick from the withdrawals, but I also had a deeper peace that was beyond the anguish. It was really awkward for me. I had never experienced anything like it before! This peace I had was detached from the present physical pain; however, it calmed and strengthened me to manage the situation I was in.

Somehow that peace gave me the sense that God had me right where He intended me to be! Later that day I broke down in front of my wife, which I never had done before. She seemed really aggravated with me and said, "Again, your feeling sick? How long is this supposed to go on?" It just crushed me even more to hear her say this, and I knew right then I just lost the last bit of support I had on earth. She was the only one who knew what I was going through, the only person on earth I could talk to truthfully just told me (without really saying it) she was no longer interested in listening to all my sad stories. I knew I deserved it. I put her through so much, and now she also had to deal with the consequences of my mistakes! I had a choice to be upset at her for not being very supportive, but God began showing me right then that she was taken out of the equation as a part of His plan, not hers! It was to bring me into complete reliance on Jesus and only Him. He was ready to give me a glimpse of His fuller mercy and His even deeper grace in my life, but first He would see to it that no one would take credit for it but Him; it would be His doing and only His doing! Wow, there was just something about knowing and sensing that His hand was involved in all the details. It was that deep peace I sensed again, through all the turmoil there was this unshakable steadiness holding me up, keeping me in place when all I wanted to do is jump ship. As contradicting as it sounds is as real as it was. His strength was being made perfect through my weakness! The weaker I got, the stronger He made me!

It's important for me to portray clearly all the while I felt His hand on me; I also felt a battle brewing up in me. The war of giving myself over to the addiction or giving myself over to Jesus was a daily battle. The temptation to give into the drugs continued. I just had a renewed strength and peace each day to overcome the temptation!

The Lord spoke to me again that weekend, and He answered me even more directly about why I was not experiencing the kind of miracle I asked for. I prayed to just never need the pills again and to have no withdrawals, and I believed for it too. I see now that faith alone is not the single formula to an answered prayer, especially when my first prayer was God's will for my life, not my own. I was driving in my car on the way home from the store thinking of why I had to feel this pain—my legs were aching, I was sweating terribly and feeling I might vomit any second. I had my kids with me, and I needed to be strong and do my best to keep appearances. My kids could tell something wasn't right, but I explained to them that I was very sick and left it at that. As I was still driving, I was asking the Lord why I had to do this any further, why couldn't He just heal me and let me feel good again. I witnessed the things He had done for me earlier in the year, why not again? I turned on the radio being restless; it was tuned to the local Christian radio station. At the very second it came on, the radio host said to a woman guest, "So you wrote this book why?"

She replied and I am paraphrasing, "Although I had to go through this very tough time in my life, and as difficult as it was, Jesus showed me, though I would go through this tough time, in the end I may share the experience and be an inspiration to others in my situation. She wrote the book for that reason! Chills ran down my spine, I mean how many times can these things happen before I have to stop saying it's just a coincidence? I knew after listening to the rest of the show that God had spoke to my heart that I would experience this time of withdrawals and pain only to use it as an encouragement for others who are in the position I was in. I knew that God had a heart of compassion for the lost, not just drug addicts but all of His children who were wandering blinded, in the dark. But first they had to know they could ask God just like

I needed to know I could ask Him; the thought He would use me to share that message was exciting! Suddenly the pain was subsiding, and the natural endorphins were pumping! I felt pretty good for a person in deep withdrawal. He let me taste this bit of freedom, and it was what I needed; even if for just one moment, it helped me see that brighter days were to come for me and that I would feel good again if I just stayed the course. This had a very powerful impact on my way of thinking, another building block He gave me just in time. It truly was the Lord who enabled me to be this man during this whole time. Looking back, I just cannot comprehend how I was able to drive, work, and talk with others without completely melting down; this was the strength that Jesus gave me, that inner peace I received was His Holy Spirit working in me the whole time. Jesus had already provided me this miracle. I just needed help to see it clearly! Throughout this experience, the Lord blessed me with several experiences, which built my faith and kept me focused on Him.

Chapter 12

Man shall not eat by bread alone . . .

I was now a good three weeks into the withdrawals from OxyContin and on a considerable lower dose of methadone, only taking a small fraction of what was prescribed to me. One evening, I was feeling so sick I had gone to bed very early. I snuck into my room exhausted from three weeks of sleepless nights and hard days. I just lay in my bed screaming inside. My mind began playing tricks on me, or maybe better yet, Satan was playing tricks on my mind. I kept telling myself that I could take extra methadone and no one would know. I would sleep so well if I would take some extra. I told myself I could start back in the morning on the taper. I wanted so badly to give in, but I also pondered the consequences of the failure I would surely face come morning. I had started out at 100 mg of methadone daily and had tapered my way down to 30 or 40 mg daily by the third week. To date I had not cheated the taper. But for some reason, it was sounding really good to me to cheat, right then the thoughts were going through my head so quickly it was hard to think clear at all. It was becoming a literal torture for me to resist the extra pill. The thought of sleeping through the night and feeling better was so appealing to me. I was just about to give in, as I rose out of bed to take a dose, when I suddenly recalled a portion of the New Testament I had read. Jesus was being tempted by Satan. He had been fasting for forty days and He was very hungry. After forty days, this was not just a little hungry but very hungry, even hungry to the point of death. But Jesus knew the Father God had a much different plan for him and it was not death by starvation. I began to compare His temptation to desire food to my temptation to take a pill. I began to see the story in my mind—Satan appeared to Jesus, tempted Him to turn stone into bread, and Jesus replied, "It is written, 'Man shall not live by bread alone, but by every word that proceeds from the mouth of God'" (Matt. 4:4)! I smiled a bit as I applied His answer to Satan's lie in my situation right then.

Then I began thinking and visualizing the story as Satan tempted Jesus again, testing His obedience to the Father's love. Satan called for Jesus to cast Himself down, and I saw that it would have been the same thing for me if I would have taken that extra pill. But again Jesus replied, "It is written . . . You shall not tempt the Lord your God" (Matt. 4:7). I smiled some more as I applied it to my situation, my confidence again grew bolder. Then Satan tried again; he asked Jesus to worship him and he would give him all the land and kingdoms of the world. Jesus replied, "Away with you, Satan! For it is written, 'you shall worship the Lord your God, and Him only you shall serve'" (Matt. 4:10). I thought of Jesus having no other gods before Him. I too wanted no other gods before Him, so I yelled out loud, "Flee Satan!"

I was so surprised how I was able to recall these Scriptures in my time of need. They were speaking life directly to my soul. I was really enjoying this newfound ability to remember the Word of God and use it so effectively. I now know it was the Holy Spirit empowering me and teaching me. It was all so clear! I just sat there for a moment awestruck. I had completely forgotten about the pills, and I was feeling so calm and confident right then. I was literary laughing out loud; the miserable state I was in was gone! Just then when I thought I couldn't be any more blessed, the good Lord brought more to my memory . . . the Bible says after Jesus overcame the temptations, after Satan had left Jesus, angels appeared and ministered to Him! Well, that did it for me; I immediately started to laugh again, quite uncontrollably! If my wife had heard me, she would have thought I had finally lost it! I laughed for about a half hour. The whole time I felt no withdrawals, at all! I guess you could say that my body's natural painkillers were working well. I believe I was laughing at how I just used the Word of God to overcome the hardest of my temptations. The thought of taking that extra pill no longer appealed to me! When I finally calmed down and thought for a moment about His ministering angels, I realized the reason the Bible tells us the angels ministered to Jesus is so we can see that there is a sweet reward for us who stand on God's Word without falter. Although we do face temptations and maybe even feel like giving in at times, perseverance through and with the Word of God is a serious weapon at our fingertips. I knew beyond a doubt, then and there, that His angels were sent to minister to me by helping me laugh a little and bringing me to a place of comfort. This is how they ministered to my spirit, and a laugh was exactly what I really needed to feel better. To some it may seem like a very little thing to have just gotten a laugh out of it, but it was exactly what I needed, at the right time and in the right place. Not only did it make me feel better, but it provided me with more skills and a new tool on how to fight future temptations. In reflection, what was really amazing to me is how my memory, which was poor in so many areas, especially in my condition during this time, that I could remember these scriptures. I never even tried to memorize them, but at the specific time I needed to hear them, they came to mind, yes I also knew this was another miracle. Here I was going through the toughest battles of my life. I was tired, under great stress, and quite agitated. I wasn't even close to the ideal condition needed for my memory to be working so well, yet I could remember scriptures I had previously read over months earlier! Add to that the fact the scriptures I would recall, related to what exactly I needed to hear at the moment I needed to hear them. Because of the impeccable timing of these memories, they were having a maximum impact on me and my faith. Praise God!

To this very day and probably for as long as I live, just thinking of this experience is very uplifting for me; the thought that Jesus loved me enough to send to me His word, His ministering angels and let me feel the reward of His love in my life shakes me up. It cuts right through all the worries of failure I've ever had. Any fear that arises I can look at this experience and recall what He has done for me. It is so very comforting. To read the Word of God is awesome, more than that was to be able to apply it in the specific instance in my life is probably the most rewarding experience I have ever had as a believer in Christ. Through all the pains and heartaches I went through to this date, it was all worth it to be able to have Jesus Christ work with me so personally by using His own life experience on this earth. Allowing me to apply it in mine was amazing, and then to allow His angels to minister to my soul by letting me laugh myself to sleep brings a joy to my spirit I cannot explain. It gave me all the strength and will I needed right then to carry on and allow him to continue His work in me.

Chapter 13

By the fourth week, I wasn't doing much better in the way of withdrawals; little did I know I had many more excruciating days ahead. I did begin to realize I was not going to do this taper as quickly as I first had thought. I had to maintain work and home, so I took it slow but was still very slowly heading down or staying at the same dosage to adjust, never once upward. Worries were creeping in, I was feeling concerned with this delay, nor was I sure I could find the strength to continue. I also felt inside the Lord was okay with it, and I believe it was His way of having my full attention long enough for me to realize I was completely at His mercy and will, not my own. This was His plan and His schedule. All along I had hoped and prayed to get it done by the fourth week;

and at that point, short a different kind of miracle, it was not going to happen without a hospital bed and time off work. If that were to happen my secret would be out, not an option for me at this point, it just was not an option. I began to fear the whole taper (again) and to think about failure and how awful it would be to fail. What would my wife think of me if I gave up? I knew I owed my kids better than this. I just felt like I could not go on for months like my doctor had first suggested. The thought of going month after month this way was overwhelming and frightening. I knew on my own, I was just not strong enough; there was no way I could continue unless God worked daily miracles in my life, there just was no way. I began thinking to myself you may be doing well today, but you'll fail, you'll see.

I thought, "Why don't I just get it over with today, why torture myself any longer just to fail another day." I asked myself, "why not fail today and be done with this pain?" I was terrified of the thought, but I kept on thinking it into early morning. I was literally torturing myself. I lied awake in bed thinking myself into a failure. One thing I learned is how powerful the mind really is, either for me or against me it can go either way depending on how I think, positive in Christ or negative in the world. It was my choice. I knew I needed to pray for skill on how to master my thoughts and stay positive in Christ even when it does not look good for me. It was about 3:00 a.m. and I was praying for peace and sleep when I heard a voice in my spirit speak to me saying, Deuteronomy 7:9. I had read a few portions of the Old Testament, but I had not yet read Deuteronomy. As I lay in bed, I was questioning myself and my sanity. I sarcastically told myself, "You can't be serious; now scriptures are just going to start popping out of you?" I tried to convince myself that Deuteronomy 7:9 probably didn't even exist in the Bible. On the other hand, I was also aware of God's mighty hand in my life as of recently. I was aching and restless, so I got up out of bed and quite reluctantly went into my living room and opened my Bible to Deuteronomy 7:9. I learned that night very clearly to take my prayers more seriously because I just might get what I asked for—peace and some sleep. I read about The Faithful God!

"Therefore know, that the Lord your God, He is God, <u>the faithful God</u> that keeps His covenant and mercy for a thousand generations with those who love Him and keep His commandments."

Deuteronomy 7:9

I just sat there silently thinking David had the faith to proclaim that God would deliver him and trust Him in his time of great need. I can rely on the fact that my God is GOD! There is nothing He cannot do and further He's *faithful* to do it. Like when He ministered to me by helping me laugh, He showed His mercy on my situation. He'll keep His promise, He'll do it mercifully, and I will receive it. I also saw something else that struck me profoundly. I remember hearing a preaching on generational curses and how they are passed from generation to generation, the thought of my kids doing what I was doing was not an option. I wasn't only afraid they would take pills or drugs but lead the life I had led with the drugs and drinking, the lies, the filth, giving up on myself and my family instead of standing up in Christ. I was not willing to accept that. I knew the curse I had was brought on me by the bad choices I made and it needed to end here; instead of a curse on my future generations, I would receive His promise. God would see to the promise I have in Him from generation to generation to come. The results of this obedience to Him! Meaning the addiction had to go, and I knew it meant one thousand generations of mine would receive a blessing by God—that's His promise and He's faithful to keep His promise!

I sat there pondering what this scripture really meant to me, my situation. I was feeling much more positive at this time, but I still had not dealt with the time frame issues of this taper. I just wanted it done and over with right then, and it was not happening quickly enough, much to my dislike. I was still very tired but still unable to sleep. I picked the Bible back up and decided to read Deuteronomy 7:9 in its context. I read about Egypt and how the Lord had delivered them! Verse 17 says, "If you should say in you heart these nations are greater than I then how shall I dispossess them?" I needed to think success was obtainable not failure . . . nothing was too big for God to overcome. God was telling me to use my mind in a positive manner, to have faith in His faithfulness.

He'll take my faith and use it to my advantage! He was saying if I should say in my heart these pills are greater than He, then how shall He dispossess them! Then I read through to verse 22, which says, "The Lord will drive out those nations before you little by little, you will be unable to destroy them at once, lest the beast of the field become too numerous for you." I had my concerns answered right then. Yes, God is faithful! He is also all-knowing and He knows me all too well. I never would have succeeded this journey all at once, and it was His will for me to succeed. And He led me through little by little lest I would be overwhelmed by my addiction, withdrawals, and all the lies from the powers and principalities of darkness. He spoke to my heart, and then I remembered something I had read in the New Testament, but I never understood.

You don't pour new wine into an old wine sack or the old sack will burst and the wine will be lost. I instantly knew what it meant for my situation. It seemed to me that the new wine was like me, and the newfound life in Christ I had and the old wine sack was a heavy burden or like my long-standing problem. And I needed to make it through in the order God had prescribed so all would not be lost—like the wine was when it spilled. Taking this new life I had found in Christ and overloading it with too much pressure from all corners may have been a prescription for disaster for me (no pun intended). I just felt that the Holy Spirit was revealing the Word of God to me and at the same time it helped me; it was also teaching me about the secrets of God! If I were to drive any one point fully, it would be that there is nothing on earth that can compare to having Jesus personally teach you, care for you, and comfort you. I am not talking about people teaching, caring, and comforting . . . I am talking about Jesus Himself doing it. These experiences were getting so incredible it just left me perpetually thirsty for more of Him. It was showing me how very powerful the Word of God is, a tool that *must be used*. Moments earlier I was in dire fear; then I read the Word of God and I am in peace! Not only was this good for victory over pills, but it cultivated me into a stronger man than I ever was. Mental strength had never been my real strongpoint, but I could see how that could easily change with Christ in my life.

Chapter 14

I had no previous knowledge of the Bible other than the children stories that were pretty much meaningless to me as a kid because I never really applied them. Suddenly I was being overwhelmed with the presence of God, and I loved it! The next thing I remembered was waking up on my couch with the Bible on the table. I actually slept a few hours, and sleep was desperately needed that night! I could clearly see God had mercy on me again, and He was faithful, He kept His promise and strengthened me to face another day. It was becoming very apparent to me by this time that God had etched in stone a victory and to destroy the pull of my addiction. No matter how hard it was going to be, I had victory in Jesus!

Let me still admit, as fantastic as the Lord was with me I was still in tremendous withdrawals and quite alert to feeling them. The mornings always began with Christ and were always met with the opposing deep depressive thoughts. Thoughts of how I'll never be happy again, aching joints like I never felt aching in my life and never to care again, excessive yawning, sneezing, fatigue, sweating, speeding heart rates, cramps, and on and on. To be candid, the symptoms completely overwhelmed me; it was difficult to stay the course, I had to constantly remind myself of what Jesus had shown me in days past, and how beautiful it was each time it happened.

Throughout the whole experience I always had that inner peace and an inner strength to press through. I know in times past I never could or would have made it this far, no way. I had surrounded myself with Jesus. All day Christian radio in my car, in my excavator, and on the job sites, despite the strange looks I'd get from time to time. I had countless Christian worship songs and inspirational CDs for when I wasn't listening to preaching. At night I read the Bible and prayed in my bedroom. I found myself back in the New Testament because the second half of the Old Testament got too tough for me to stay focused. The Lord revealed things to me during this time just when I really needed them most. It always seemed at my weakest moments I would have a breakthrough of some sort and gain some strength to go another day. Day after day I fed on His Word and was given the Bread of Life. Literally hand-fed like a baby. I believe I was fed by Jesus

Christ Himself. Keeping this a secret meant I had no one else I could turn to—to talk about my fears, get spiritual advice, only Jesus was my source. Each night I would come home and look forward to the fact that I could rest my joints and not have to worry about the pain while doing my job. Coming home at night was the highlight of my day for that very reason. Every night I walked through the door I just had to praise God that somehow I didn't fall back into old habits and was able keep the course God had laid out for me.

I was given strength on what I called "an as needed basis." Not too much so I didn't get too smart for my own good, but enough to succeed, all the while being able to really see and feel the consequences of what I had done to myself all these years. As much as I wanted to give up, the excitement of success won out each day. How can I put this into words other than to say, I can assure you this was just a miracle, plainly and unexplainable any other way, a miracle of mighty proportions! The first time I tried withdrawal years earlier I went to one of the best rehabs in New England. I had all the fancy medications and daily doctor and nurse supervision. My own private hospital bed, I did not have to work or worry about anything; but my well-being and I ultimately failed, left for home on medication, and within no time was worse than when I started out in the rehab center. But this time it was working. I had no doctor supervision or any fancy meds to make life a little more bearable, all the while I managed to work each day but

Sundays. What I truly had was Jesus Christ in my life, and I wanted Him to have all the glory for this. Because I had this secret, giving glory to God was difficult because I was unable to share it with anyone other than my wife. But I praised Him and thanked Him personally for His work in me all the time. One of the best parts of what Jesus was doing for me, and I don't think I even understood at the time, was this: Jesus and I were building a personal relationship together through this time. It was like meeting a person for the first time—you see things you admire in one another, you spend more time together, one thing leads to another, and before you know it you're the best of friends, inseparable. Before long this best friend becomes a major a part of you and your life. I felt this about Jesus, together we became inseparable. I knew when the time was right for God to take the glory He'd let me know, after all He let me know everything else I never knew before right when I needed to know it; meanwhile, it was a well-kept secret among best friends.

Chapter 15

By now I was getting into my third month of withdrawal. I was starting to get pretty accustomed to the withdrawal and ways to deal with it. I was not really feeling too well, but not feeling terribly bad either. What I had been doing was dropping my dose about 5 mg. Every two to three weeks or so down until I got to 10 mg per day. I felt like I had this under control and was very close to being done. So much so that on a couple of occasions I decided to try not taking my morning dose and see how I'd do. By 10:00 A.M. I was physically destroyed by withdrawals, just as bad as the first day. I remember how sick it made me feel both physically and mentally. The mental part was worse because I was feeling like I had so far to go on the physical end of it. I got so scared. So I turned to the Internet to research some remedies or to read other stories of people who were in my situation. It was the worse thing I ever could have done. I pretty much scared myself back into a full-blown addiction. I was horrified of the stories people shared. Some were countless years' later still fighting. Scores of doctors writing articles saying that methadone is a medicine to a drug addict like insulin is to a diabetic. They claimed that this was a sickness or disease, and methadone was my prescription for that disease that could only be managed—not cured! That it was not something I needed to be ashamed of. I read posting after posting of how people tried time and time again and in the end always failed. I read about rapid detox under anesthesia and how dangerous it was and you still had withdrawals anyway. It all came down to there was just no hope for me in the world. As I was getting off the Internet, I stopped at one more doctor's Web site and wrote a message to him about my withdrawal pain and asked him why I was so sick still. I felt that I was on such a low dose of methadone that I would be able to just stop at that point. He wrote me back the next day. I can't quote him, but he basically said this. He had done over a one hundred detox programs for his patients, and the withdrawal from 1 mg of methadone was just as bad as cold turkey from 100 mg. Adjusting to a lower dose was much different than losing the dose all together because of the way it deposits itself into your tissues. He said no matter how much I had tapered down I was still in for a world of hurt. He recommended some special vitamins and medicine for the long haul to help with the rebuilding of my brain chemicals, but other than that, I was pretty much crushed and very scared to look ahead. I do not know if my failure to keep my eyes on Jesus was because of my body's depressed state, or if I was just stiff-necked like the Jews were, or both.

I do know this. I never should have taken my eyes off Jesus because I was doing fine under His supervision, and now I was horrified and ready to quit right then. I knew what Jesus had done for me up to this point was real, but I began to think that maybe I wasn't ready for the full commitment of this. This was Satan trying to sidetrack me before my victory. I began to think to myself Jesus will forgive me, after all I am just a sinner like anyone else. Even if I conquered this I would still be a sinner, and Jesus would forgive me so what is one more sin. I had perfectly, 100 percent rationalized my ability to sin and be forgiven in just moments. I was ready to call my doctor and get a new prescription, and that was pretty much it. All that work for nothing. I went into my medicine cabinet and looked for whatever was in it besides methadone and found one Vicodin pill from an old dental surgery I had a year earlier. I had not used it because then I had more powerful medication to deal with a little tooth surgery. I took the Vicodin and went out the door to work. About an hour later, I found myself actually smiling on a job site. I wasn't euphoric from it, but it felt so good to feel better; it was really scary. A few months earlier I could have taken an entire bottle of these and would not have been fazed, and now one pill had an effect on my personality and my aches and pains. I began to rationalize this even more. I could forgo the OxyContin and methadone and go straight to Vicodin, after all Vicodin was a lesser narcotic than the other, and it made me feel good. I thought then if I wanted, I could just taper off them when I was ready. I knew all I had to do was call my doctor for the script and it was done. He'd be happy to prescribe these to me over the other drugs any day. Besides, he never figured me for success anyway, I thought to myself. I guess my doctor was right about me. Sadly I thought I had it all figured out. But it wasn't over yet.

I am convinced at this point in my life that I may have just liked torturing myself! I was doing so well and bang I was willing to start this all up again just like that. I dialed my doctor's number so many times and hung up before it rang for a week straight. It taunted me, but I could not seem to make that call. Something just pulled me away each time I tried to make the call. The conviction of the Holy Spirit is really powerful when it wants to be. Basically, Jesus was telling me, "You are weak but I am strong!" I remember reading Jesus' words saying, *My strength is made perfect through your weakness.* I recalled what the apostle Paul wrote for us, to keep our minds focused on the things of God, things that are true and trustworthy, praiseworthy . . . and I knew I had to do this. I looked back over my experiences and remembered the experience I had with Jesus and focusing on His face. I knew I had to look for the face of Jesus or I'd be doomed to fail. I had walked out of the light of Jesus and looked into the darkness of the world for answers. Just the one little, tiny simple time I had to wander on the Internet for my needs, and WHAM I was ready to give up and start a whole new narcotic drug, which would have lead to worse I am sure of it.

Just like when I left the detox on a lower dose and ended up worse than before. That same week I heard a teaching on radio about when a demon leaves a person, he returns to find the house swept up and in order, so he goes out and brings seven more demons with him, and the state of that person will be worse than when he started. I just could not do it. I knew when I left rehab years earlier I was on a small dose of a new drug, and my problem went from bad to worse within months, what it would be this time if I gave up. I believe overdose would have been my next stop. As simple as it is to say "I could not do it," it's just not a fair understanding of that statement. I wanted to do it so badly! I felt the desire to give in deep down at times to the point my mouth watered at the thought of it, and once my mouth watered with desire, it took days to get over that one bad thought. Thanks be to Jesus, day after day I came home and by His grace did not do it. As for the Vicodin, I took the one pill that day and never touched one again. I tortured myself with both mental withdrawals as well as physical ones because of my look to man for my answers and the consequences were brutal, but they could have been much worse. In reflection, I believe that surrounding myself with the things of

God was what pulled me through this time and the others also. I had so many uplifting times from Jesus that the momentum from these experiences and the joy they gave me pushed me through even when I seemed to come to a complete stop personally with Him. God knew my heart's desire was for Him, and He stepped in at my weakest times every time!

Chapter 16

Behold, I will do a new thing, now it shall surely spring forth; shall

you not know it?

Isaiah 43:19

I noticed that whenever God stepped in, it seemed like I was right at the last second before failure. He was never early or late with His help, just right on time, every time. It's almost like in the movies when the a man is about to lose his last finger grip on the edge of high building and the hero swoops in just as that man lets go and grabs his wrist just at that same moment. It seems to me that maybe I needed to dance dangerously close to the edge so I could look down and see the fall before He'd catch me. That way there I'd have no doubt it was God Himself who saved me, obviously not me or anyone else and definitely not some Internet doctor that I had never met before!

So I got past the whole Vicodin problem, but I was still having the thoughts of what the doctor told me about the severe withdrawals I had coming. It really scared me to think that I had not experienced the full pain yet and wouldn't until I was going from a few milligrams to none. I thought, "If what I had been feeling all these months was not the worse, then what could be worse?" I was terrified of what I would do for work during that time, and I questioned what would people think if they found out? I had a host of thoughts that plagued my mind and kept me bewildered. I needed to recall Deuteronomy 7:9 and I did . . . "Know that I am God the Faithful God that keeps his promise."

Whether it is my addiction or any other problem that seemed impossible for me, I had to remember and believe that God is God and that is that. It was a real simple statement for me. It was like saying the sky is blue on a clear day because it is blue. It is not yellow or brown; it is blue. This is a very simple statement as I saw it. God is God, and He's faithful. If you believe in the Father God, the Son Jesus, and the Holy Spirit, then what is there to worry about? He's God and anything is possible, and He's faithful to do it! Just then I had another divine revelation about Jesus when He scolded His disciples in the Garden of Gethsemane when they kept falling asleep instead of being on alert for Him; He warned them to be watchful and said, "Indeed the spirit is willing but the flesh is weak." My spirit was so willing, and my flesh was very weak. I had to stay alert and be watchful for things of the world that are destined to come against me. This was and still is a way for me to protect myself from being sucked into the matters of the world. I needed to get back to basics. For me basics were if you believe in your heart He is real, then call upon Jesus and He will guide your path. Proverbs 3:5-6 says, "Trust in the Lord with all your heart, and lean not on your own understanding, in all your ways acknowledge Him, and He shall direct your paths!" I took this thinking and applied it to my problem, and it worked simply because God is God and He kept His promise to me. At this point it became clearer that a full victory was inevitable, and that was powerful, positive thinking that built my faith up (again) to begin working on the plan to finish what Jesus started in me.

Before I had done anything, I had been praying and seeking for when it would be my time to finish this. I knew by now it was not going to be my timing. I had already tried my timing, and I saw what happened. It was when Jesus was ready for me to make that step to victory and not a minute sooner. I remember when He spoke to me very clearly, I was sitting at my desk doing some typing and when I received an e-mail from a Jewish Christian preacher about a new work God was doing with His saints. As I read on, I sensed this was a nudge from God to move forward. I said "yes" to myself and then prophesized to myself "Behold a new season has come, a season for victory, a season for prosperity, and a season of new heights and in this season you will give glory to God." I sensed the peace and power of the Holy Spirit coming through. I could never make times like this happen to me, they just happened; and when they did, I knew it was from God. It had His name all over it. I felt uplifted, but I have to admit there was worry in my mind because I knew it was time to go the rest of the way. That evening I lay in bed praying to Jesus and wondering how I would do it. Suddenly, I had this thought that just ran through my mind: *From here, your Father God will take you through, and He will do His work in you and it will not be harder, it will be easier, and it will be quick.* I liked that thought very much! I felt like He said to me you've had faith, now watch My grace really work in you, there will be an abundance of grace, more than you've experienced or seen so far! I was still very scared; I needed this badly. The fear of feeling this pain as the Internet doctor had informed me had been in the back of my mind all this time, and this word that ran through my mind just countered that with a positive Word from God.

That was what I had hung my hat on, and it was sufficient to begin the process. I will not lie. I still had the haunting thoughts of what to expect, but I was uplifted enough by God's Word for me to leave behind these depressive thoughts and not to allow them to stay with me. I knew what God had already done with me and I wasn't able to forget it.

It was Friday, March 17, 2006, that was the last day I took a pill from my bottle. By noontime I was sweating bullets and rubbing my kneecaps to beat the band. I should mention I was sweating and rubbing my kneecaps while I worked because I made it through the day relatively well, considering all that was going on. I knew my last methadone dose could work on withdrawals in a body for up to thirty-six hours and can settle in your tissues for even longer. The real test would be making it to that coming Tuesday morning. Saturday was long and I was quite irritable, but I managed it without making much of a scene. I did not have to work that day, so I was able to just crawl off into a corner and hide. I had absolutely no intentions to go to church the next morning; but when the time came, I showered, dressed, and made my way very slowly. I thought I was melting during the service, but other than that, I survived it fine. After church, my parents came over for lunch and coffee, and I thought I'd burst out crying when I heard they were on their way. I just wanted to sleep my last day off that weekend, but I managed it fine and got my sleep later on in the day.

I guess I was very apprehensive that I was fully on my way to success, but inside I knew I really was. Deep inside, I was holding my breath and thanking God at the same time. I know it sounds contradictory to hold my breath and thank God simultaneously, but that is the truth. I believe God saw my heart and my desire, and forgave me of my fears while He worked in me. He saw my fears, but His grace also noted my faith. He was my strength to overcome all fear, the inner peace I had all along was His Holy Spirit in me working! In past years all I saw was God as the punishing God, now all I could see Him as was the all-merciful and understanding God. It was so funny how confident I was in His understanding of my weakness. After all, this was the absolute hardest thing I had ever done so far in my life. I pondered what Jesus really meant when He said His strength was made perfect in my weakness! It was simple for me to see clearly at that point; meaning you could never experience His perfect strength unless you were weak! I was weak—I needed His strength. This scripture made me feel better about my weakness, especially when I could expect His perfect strength to follow!

Chapter 17

That Monday morning is when I really knew that God had really spoken to me when my son ran up to me and said, "Dad, did you know today is the first day of a new season?" I replied, "No, I did not." He said, "Yeah, Dad, my teacher said today is the first day of Spring!" I remember looking outside and seeing the wind howling through the rear yard and snow blowing all around and thinking it can't be Spring today. Just then the morning-news weatherman said something to the effect that it may not feel like it, but today is the first day of Spring! He was right it did not feel like a new season for me, but I recalled God had spoke to me and said it was a new season for me. I was ready to stand by His Word for me—it was a new season. I went out to face the day with a boost of faith and strength. Proclaiming, "Today is a new season!"

Wouldn't you know that of all times, when I am finalizing the taper, I got a call from a good customer who had two one-day jobs he needed done right away; they just could not wait. I was hoping for a simple week, nothing complicated. I wasn't impressed with the short notice and the pressure to begin immediately. I almost refused the work. I had not done a job for this company for several months, and all of the sudden two at one time? I was already busy on a regular scheduled job, but I really liked this man and wanted to help, so I agreed to do them. So the pressure was on to keep the regular scheduled work satisfied while meeting the needs of the new emergency jobs.

I found myself running all over town shuffling this and fitting in that, hauling this here and then over there and so on. At the time it seemed like a real hassle to have to do this, but come Tuesday afternoon I realized how fast time has slipped on by! I was so consumed by my work I was unable to fixate on the withdrawals! I made it past that all important three days and onto the fourth day from the day I last took a dose! It felt so good to be at that stage where I could just say it was *finally* over. I still had the yawning, sneezing, and a little aching; but each day was actually getting easier. Easier was really sweet music to my spirit. I really liked the easier part! Then I got to thinking, *Wait a minute here, that internet doctor said I would have the same terrible withdrawals from 100 mg versus 1 mg.* I guess he was wrong . . . or maybe he was right? Maybe it was my faithful God who carried me through the last bit of the way! He put His hand on me once again and made a way for me. The Bible does say He'll even bring the mountains low, cause streams to flow in the desert, and make our crooked paths straight (Isaiah 41:18, 42:16, 43:19)! It was God all right! As the Bible says:

"So you shall know that I am the Lord your God" (Joel 3:17)!

So the physical addiction had been addressed, but I for ten years developed a mental addiction also, even to the point my mouth would water at the thought of a pill. I remain clean and I have no earthly desire within me to touch, to look, and definitely to take a pill ever again. Just the thought of going back to that life would be worse than the withdrawals itself. I realize that if I lost sight of Jesus, then I would be vulnerable to relapse or develop other addictions. I know I have to keep my eyes on Jesus. Today (March 2005) as I am writing this paragraph, I am less than three weeks clean of these pills. I am still at what experts would call a very vulnerable point for relapse. Where the mental effects of the addiction began to play the tricks on your head, and you start to feel like life it's so lame without the drug and what will you ever do without the high. And at your weakest moment you give in just that one time, and it was all for nothing. I am here to say that I do not feel vulnerable because Jesus showed me so many secret places where I can run for cover and protection; He was showing me what happens when I leave His secret place and look to the world for answers. I know it is up to me to stay in the secret place or leave it. I realize I need this secret place of our Father because He was my strength in the past, He is my strength today, and He'll continue to be my strength tomorrow because He is God and He is faithful. He is who was, He is who is, and He is who is to come!

Chapter 18

Seven Years later!

Of course, I know while on earth we are all subject to the lies from powers and principalities of Satan, but I stand ready to battle with the armor that I learned to use through the words and life of Jesus. Had I been healed like I wanted to be, that is instantly, I never would have learned about all these tools I have at my disposal for temptations. I never would have had the awesome experiences I had. Most importantly, I never would have developed such a rich and personal relationship with Jesus. Looking back, I can say I am glad it went the way it did. Taking a look back at my whole life, I cannot help but notice some details that will always stick out to me. Having Christian parents was very helpful, but more than that made the difference for me. If I had not seen that vision of Mary with Jesus that evening while sleeping in my parents' room, I never would have been attracted to pray in the first place. My life as a teenager went off in its own direction and my Christian family could not stop it. I developed an unhealthy fear of God; it came to the point of contempt. I had an attitude that despised Him and even began doubting in the reality of Him altogether. However, seeing that vision never left my mind because it was so real, and it was truly like looking right at someone, like seeing someone face-to-face—it was just too real to ignore. Looking back, I could ask God, "Why did you let me see that? Didn't you know that it would scare the pants off me?" Scared as I was, I am glad it happened because it planted a seed of belief deep inside my soul that just needed that first drink of water and that little bit of sunlight to grow.

Knowing about God all my life was good, but having never experienced what believing in Christ was all about was what I lacked and desperately needed. Running off to Florida as a young teenager set in motion another chain of events that today, looking back, resulted in circumstances that lead me to see what I was doing to myself, being as blind as I was before this experience. I mentioned my neck was fractured possibly at birth and reinjured at the height of my business and youth. I believe from birth God knew I would experience this challenge in my life. Even though having fractures in my neck was painful, the pain was not allowed to make me suffer, nor do I believe God was the cause. Rather God, foreknowing my difficulties in a fallen creation turned it for my good, ultimately leading me, my wife and kids to truly see Jesus for who He is, our Savior in every way. Despite my problems, He was still my God! I was never going to be saved on my own doing. I had to ask, "Why would saving me from my misery be so important to Him." Being predestined to a path does not mean I did not have choices to make on my own, but the opportunities God made for me to escape the troubles were always right there! I just kept missing them.

It is not like God has this factory production line, and as I passed by, He stamped my forehead with the road map of my life; it was much more than that, He blessed me with a life full of opportunity, knowing full well I'd fail Him over and over again. I believe that my finding the Lord, no matter what way it happened, is the most important thing of all my testimony because I am sure He has a purpose for me. One that will ultimately further His kingdom and bring Him glory!

This whole experience has caused me to look further at my circumstances I face each day. To face the different challenges of life the way Christ would, not they way I'd sometimes like. If I do give into my flesh, and at times I still do, I have missed another opportunity God had for me. I have to keep reminding myself of that when I do miss one. I know through experience how rewarding an opportunity from God can be! I also realize His opportunities are not always easy, but they are all rewarding, the reward that comes after the choosing of the right opportunity provided. The great part I can say for sure, being a person who has missed so many of His opportunities, is that God is long suffering, and He will continue as long as you're alive on this earth to give you them. He works all things together for good, for those who love Him and are called according to His purpose…. Just His long-suffering alone shows His grace, not to mention the actual opportunity provided is His grace at even higher proportions. I have concluded that His love is bigger than anyone can explain or comprehend. My biggest prayer at this point in my life is that I will stay aware of His next opportunity for me, and I will live a life that brings the kingdom of God glory.

Thinking of opportunity, God provided me the chance to change my life and come clean, which led me to Jesus. By knowing Jesus, I am made a better man, a better husband, and a better father. I will strive to lead my children in the things of God, and instead of my children being raised fatherless, they may now one day play an important role in the kingdom of God. Before any of this happens, I recall that my wife was somewhat mixed up and confused, no doubt by what I put her through. Now I see her interacting with a church for the first time in our marriage, and she's actually reading the Bible on her own doing for the first time. It is all so overwhelming how one vision as a child could ultimately start in motion years later such a change for my family. It is clear God had a plan for me and my family; He still has a plan for us, He has a plan for us all. It's not a plan that came together last minute. I admit I was a mess, but He had me in His hand the whole time. I may have gone astray, but He never let me out of His sight. The opportunities were always available. One way I like to think of God is as the greatest mathematician or calculus that ever existed and ever will exist. He can calculate a set of circumstances from birth to equal opportunities for you to succeed and be victorious right now. If you miss one chance, His calculations have already made another opportunity for you to jump on board. Then one day you began a relationship with Jesus Christ and your eyes are widely opened and you look around and say, "Wow, there's a whole world of God-ordained opportunities just waiting for me to move on!" I know that God wants the best for all humanity, but too often they're missed because we don't turn ourselves over completely to the face of Jesus to see them. It was the ways of the world that led me deeper and darker every day to the point I was completely lost and had no choice but to look outside of the foolish wisdom of man and straight into the face of Jesus.

I know trusting in Jesus is really hard work in the worlds view, and there are times when it takes hard work to stay the course. But we must always remember it is in our weakness that He supplies His strength!

The bible says we are saved by grace, through faith...His grace was always here, but I had to learn to take hold of it through faith in what Jesus did for me on the cross. I had to stop living under the rule of condemnation. Always recounting my wrongs, figuring myself unable to receive His goodness, and start trusting Jesus paid the price on Calvary. I had to accept that He still loved me and He indeed had good plans for me, despite my shortcomings. Even the faith to do this was His gift to me; it rushed in when I began reading the Word of God! *So then faith comes by hearing, and hearing by the word of God. (Romans 10:17)*

I also know the more you press in with saving faith, the more you align with His wonderful working power and grace, the greater the reward! For me my reward today is Jesus Christ, my salvation, total forgiveness, total freedom from a vicious addiction, an exciting joy I cannot explain, and so much more! You must experience it yourself to really appreciate these words—to take hold of that inner peace and rise up with the strength of Christ is an awesome thing! I am so very humbled to have had this opportunity to experience a depth of Jesus I had not known before. Originally, I admit I never realized what a relationship with Christ really meant to me. I had no idea going into this that I would be quitting pills and changing everything about me! It has been nothing less than the most remarkable journey I could ever desire!

As hard as overcoming the addiction was, the rewards were one thousand times better; in fact, it's been exceedingly, abundantly above all that I could have ever imagined or thought it to be!

Praise my Lord Jesus Christ I am no longer a stranger or foreigner, but a citizen of the saints and a member of the household of my Father God. I am of the sons and daughters of the Most High King, and I have part in the full inheritance in the kingdom of God!

Yes it is seven years later. No pills, no more doctors, no hospitals, no antidepressants, no sweating, no shaking, no fear— it's just all gone, quite plain and simple, *gone*. I also would like to add that after the pills, He delivered me from yet another addiction of cigarette smoking. I had been smoking for twenty-four years. When I finally quit, I was averaging three packs per day; basically, I was a chain smoker. The faithful God has stayed with me as much as the first day I found Him. He has shown me ways to cope with neck pain by using certain foods, and it works and works quite well.

I believe He has preserved me for these years from temptation as a part of His continued faithfulness to my deliverance. I have grown even closer to Him since my delivery, and He has continued to reveal Himself to me, and each time He leaves me in awe. In the past seven years, He has also blessed me beyond measure in my family, my business, my finances, my friends and has shown me some very great and mighty things!

Because of this experience, I can say these things with confidence and assurance—I know God is our Creator, our Father, He is infinite, immeasurable, sovereign, good, merciful, loving, and of course, Faithful! I can only smile when I think of Him, and I want for you to smile too.

Each time He reveals Himself to me; it's so awe-inspiring that I wonder how He can top Himself the next time. Then I think of that, and smile again while telling myself, "He'll never stop topping it!" I just need to be ready and be watchful that I am always open to receive Him.

Thank you Jesus, my Friend, my King,

my Savior and my Lord!

About The Cover

I remember really struggling what to do for a cover, I thought of sunsets, a man on the boat in the sunset, the storm clouds and so many others. I looked through countless photos, reflecting on them as I thought on God's faithfulness. How do I capture my story in a photo, I thought? I see now it was actually all so ridiculous! I was pressured by a publisher to decide and I just couldn't. One night lying in bed I remember praying for guidance. I knew God had led me to write this testimony down so I looked for guidance on the cover. I drifted off...then suddenly I was jarred and awoke speaking this: A PICTURE TAKES AWAY FROM THE MESSAGE! It distracts from the message! That bothered me at first; I didn't understand what this meant at all. As I lay there thinking, it suddenly became clear to me. I wanted this great photo to make the look of the book catchy to the eye, professional, but that wasn't what the message of this book was about. So I thought some more, asking myself, "What exactly is the message of this book?" As I pondered it all, I saw this cover clearly in my mind. Red letters "The Faithful God" over a stark white background. As I pondered this, I gained complete peace and realized this was the cover. It had absolute meaning! I was saved by the blood of Jesus, the red letters. I am cleansed white as snow, the white background! On the surface it could seem a bit tacky, but the meaning behind it was larger than life!

I sensed it was the Holy Spirit guiding and directing me and so I fashioned the cover as it is. This cover is about the message of God's faithfulness & grace, which was demonstrated in Christ's gift to wash us clean by His blood which gives us a new life! I am the new life in Christ!

THE END

and

The BEGINNING!

To see more of what God is doing in Fab's Life!

To know more about Christ in your Life!

To order more copies of this Book!

Visit us at

www.Signs4Jesus.com

You can contact Fabrizio by email at

fab.cusson@signs4jesus.com

or

thefaithfulgod@yahoo.com